4/9/24 /

WANDA

MAY YOU HIT

YOUR NEXT

BULLSEYE!

BULLSEYE!
Hitting Your Targets at Home and at Work

Jeff Blackman

AVIV
PRESS

AVIV
PRESS

979-8-9869880-2-3 - Print

979-8-9869880-1-6 - EBook

"Stories transform lives—in the telling and the retelling. Blackman's stories and lessons learned pack a punch to the gut and rivet your thinking."

—Dianna Booher, award-winning author of 49 books, including bestsellers *Communicate Like a Leader* and *Creating Personal Presence*

"I've had the pleasure of knowing Jeff for decades. And his initial bullseye story about his teenage experience with his dad, (who I also knew), lays the foundation for a series of short, yet impactful stories that'll inspire and empower you. Each, resonates in some area of your life—to help you achieve new levels of success. And to live your life with purpose. This wonderful quick-read, is a thought-provoking collection of wisdom and winning ways. It's the perfect gift for yourself, teammates, loved ones and those who are important to you. Plus, it's the ideal source for knowledge and motivation, to start or end your day."

—Dr. Nido R. Qubein • President, High Point University

"Wow! Jeff had me at the intro, because he's such a great storyteller. Plus, his warm, funny, friendly voice shines through. Readers will love Jeff's stories about Jerry Seinfeld, Bill Russell, Bruce Jenner and others. And I bawled at the story about his beloved dad. *Bullseye* is a great, quick read that delivers wisdom, experience and perspective."

—Melissa Isaacson, award-winning journalist and author of the bestselling *State: A Team, A Triumph, A Transformation*

"In his easy to read conversational style, Jeff Blackman lays out lessons that will help people live the American Dream, where the freedom we have—gives everyone the opportunity to achieve "success" based on their ability and efforts. Young people should read his inspirational stories, to learn what they can do when they dream big and work hard. I also highly recommend this book for those already launched in their careers, and for those still in school, for it will awaken an appreciation for what one can achieve, when they work hard enough for it."

—Jack Miller, Chairman • Jack Miller Center, For Teaching America's Founding Principles and History

"My business is about helping clients create amazing customer service experiences. Jeff has created an amazing reading experience! This fascinating book is loaded with inspirational and meaningful stories that deliver important life and business lessons. And it's written in Jeff's friendly, conversational and witty style. He'll make you think, laugh and take action. And he'll even take you behind-the-scenes on his conversations and experiences with some of the top achievers in the world."

—Shep Hyken, customer service/experience expert and bestselling author, *The Amazement Revolution*

"Jeff has had a positive, powerful and long-lasting impact on our company. Twice, he has spoken to our LINX team in-person. And the same passion, energy, valuable content and dynamic storytelling he brings to a "live" program—he now delivers in the pages of *BULLSEYE*—with classic, timeless wisdom!"

—Erik Isernhagen, CEO • LINX

"*Bullseye!* is engaging, entertaining and the title is perfect! Jeff powerfully uses his storytelling skills—about his life and business experiences, or interviews and time spent with celebrities and pro athletes—to drive home real-world success strategies. I really enjoyed his story about his father, who I knew personally. And I see the same exceptional qualities in Jeff. If you want to hit more bullseyes in your personal and professional lives, this is a must-read."

—Larry Kaufman, bestselling author, *The NCG Factor*

"Whenever you read a book about success and hitting targets in your life, ask yourself three questions: 1. Is the author successful? 2. Is the advice valid? and 3. Is the book well written and fun to read? When it comes to *Bullseye*, all three answers are a resounding YES! Jeff is an example of sustained success and he has written a practical, well-researched and engaging book. You'll reap the rewards when you read and apply his wisdom."

—Mark Sanborn, bestselling author, *The Fred Factor* and *The Intention Imperative*

"Jeff Blackman expertly combines his storytelling talent, plus life and business acumen, to deliver an entertaining collection of real-life stories with practical and proven lessons. A captivating, fun read with lots of takeaways from start to "finish.""

—Wayne Messmer, Ph.D., CSP / author, *The Voice of Victory* / anthem soloist & former P.A. announcer, Chicago Cubs

"Jeff Blackman's latest book, *Bullseye: Hitting Your Targets at Home and at Work*, is a wonderful mix of powerful short stories that combine wisdom and humor that will enlighten and inspire you to take positive actions. Buy it and read it today!"

—Daniel Burrus, New York Times bestselling author of seven books including *Flash Foresight* and *The Anticipatory Organization*

"How do you describe your goals? Do you see them as bullseyes? And how do you see what you can't see? These are challenges Jeff Blackman guides you through in *Bullseye!*

Along the way, you'll discover how he benefited from his embarrassments, pain, joys and triumphs. Imagine how you can hit your targets—when you leverage your vision and emotional energy."

—George Torok, podcast host of *Your Intended Message*

"I love to use Jeff's great *Bullseye Breakthroughs &
Boosters* to encourage and motivate our clients when
they might stray. It's all about successful outcomes and
they don't come without effort, creativity and
discipline. Jeff's positive lessons are wonderful and to
the point. This book helps one identify areas for
improvement, in business and life!"

—Tim Padgett, CEO & Founder • Pepper Group

"The same dynamic storytelling Jeff Blackman
superbly executes when he's speaking to an audience,
he now masterfully delivers in the printed word. His
Bullseye stories and their lessons keep you engaged,
entertained and focused. And they apply to achieving
success in your personal and professional life. Plus,
they're relevant, timely and fun to read for both young
and seasoned employees."

—Gerry LoDuca, President • Dukal

"*Bullseye* is one of the best books I've read in years.
Jeff's inspiring, real world stories of people, many of
whom we all know, share simple, yet powerful lessons.
His *breakthroughs* are clear, focused and applicable
immediately. This book will change the way you
approach your work and your life. Thank you, Jeff, for
your wisdom, sharing, and especially for reminding us
of what's truly important."

**—Barbara A. Glanz, Hall of Fame speaker and
author of 14 books, including *The Simple Truths
of Service Inspired by Johnny the Bagger* with
Ken Blanchard**

"Love this book and its style. We devoured Jeff's collection of stories and lessons. They're as upbeat and meaningful as Jeff always is—during one of his live speaking engagements. You'll laugh, you'll learn and you might cry (have tissues nearby)! *Bullseye* is a wonderful, inspiring book you can read anytime—you need to remember what matters in business and life."

—**Richard Fenton & Andrea Waltz, bestselling authors, *Go for No!***

To my many clients—
who daily, give me the privilege
to serve, learn and grow.

To Mom and my late Dad—
who are always qvelling. And who taught
me at an early age, if you do good work,
you'll succeed, but when you give
"a little extra"—you'll succeed beyond
your wildest expectations!

To my family—
my wife or "date for life" Sheryl and
our kids—Chad, Brittany and Amanda,
son-in-law Rob, and Brittany and Rob's
newborn twins Sloane and Charlie, who help
me realize the commitment to serve, help and
grow others—happens not just in your
business, but also in your home!

Contents

Introduction
Ready. Aim. Fire!

Many have told me that what I saw as a teenager on that memorable Wisconsin day in 1972 represents the things we must all hold dear in life: core values, meaningful tenets, powerful lessons to learn. Plain and simple, it's about the right stuff!

What kind of stuff? Stuff like possibilities, persistence, listening, teamwork, focus, belief, goals, and vision.

This story's start makes you smile. Even laugh. Next it tugs at your heart, then grabs your tummy. Yet most important, it'll help you consider all of life's possibilities and opportunities—to help you envision your future successes or *bullseyes!*

As a professional speaker, this story is one I've *told* for years, but for some strange reason never jotted it down . . . up 'til now! Your eyes can finally read what my eyes have treasured since the age of sixteen.

It's the type of lifetime experience you forever value. Yet it defies logic. Seems implausible or even impossible.

It's not. I saw it. Lived it. Cherish it.

In this book, I also build upon the *BULLSEYE* story with other compelling, thought-provoking, inspirational stories about life and business. Included are my personal experiences with iconic folks, like; Mark Cuban, Jerry Seinfeld, Bill Russell and other top-achievers.

Now, it's time to help you live *your* life on target and full of possibilities. As you hit your next *BULLSEYE!*

Hitting the BULLSEYE!

When I was sixteen, my dad and I took a trip to Whitewater Lake, Wisconsin. It was the chance for dad and I to do the stuff we seldom did together at home—take long walks, golf, and fish.

Now we ain't good fishermen. We're "city folk." I'll never forget what Mr. Miller, owner of the Whitewater Lodge said, "We could stock the bathtub with bass, and you city folk still wouldn't catch one!" He was right! But this trip was different. Unforgettable.

One day, after another futile fishing adventure, Dad and I pulled into the dock. In the distance, we saw a large, open, expansive area where about three hundred people had gathered. It had a carnival-like setting with family, friends, brats, brew, and games.

Now, I love games. And one game attracted the most attention. The dunk-tank. You've seen it before: a small pool of water, with a wooden plank above it. Sitting on top of the plank is often a town councilman, a politician or a local celebrity—somebody you'd like to take a "friendly shot" at.

And off to the right is a big black and white target with a red bullseye in the middle. About twenty feet in front of the dunk-tank was a line, where for only a quarter you could stand and hurl two twelve-inch softballs to "dunk the politician."

Dad and I watched with great interest, as a man approached the line. He planted his feet. He raised his head. And concentrated on the target.

His arm went down. His elbow went back. His shoulder went up. He reached and he threw...

And he missed.

Yet, he had another opportunity. Just like you too, always have another opportunity. This time, a friend stood at his side. Just like you've got friends, supporters and believers at your side.

And she repeated to him two words I'll never forget, "Higher, right. Higher, right. Higher, right." Again, his arm went down. His elbow went back. His shoulder went up. He reached and he threw...

BOOM!

He hit the bullseye! The politician shot-up and then...

SPLASH!

Three-hundred people erupted with euphoric applause, raucous laughter and heartfelt joy. Dad and I had goosebumps running down our backs.

You might be asking yourself, "What's the big deal? A guy hits a target from twenty feet away. Hundreds erupt with laughter, joy and applause. You and Dad have goosebumps. I don't get it!"

Well, there's one fact I haven't mentioned. The man who hurled that softball...

Was blind!

Now, you might be wondering, "Jeff, how can a guy hit a target he can't even see?" I ask you this question, "How can *you* hit targets, you don't even have?"

I've discovered there are two types of people in this world, there are those who stand upon the ground and look up at others to see, and then there are those who overcome a challenge and pursue an opportunity—to climb their successful tree.

Which type of person, do *you*...choose to be?

Bullseye Breakthroughs & Boosters:

So from this story, what can we learn? The lessons are many:

- Vision, doesn't require eyesight.
- Be decisive. Take action.
- Choose to become an optimist versus pessimist. This is the difference between being on-target or having just-missed. Your choice.
- Imagine your world of infinite possibilities.
- When challenged, choose to be a champion.
- Never overlook or underestimate the power of *you*.
- Refuse to quit. Your next attempt may hit the bullseye.
- Listen, especially to those who can help you.
- Live a life of possibilities. To do so, real responsibility belongs to you.

Introduction

- Take chances.
- Erase boundaries. Embrace possibilities.
- Don't put limits on your potential.
- Focus. Let no obstacle deter you from your goal.
- Live a life of no regrets.
- Expect victory.

May you always hit your targets—at home and at work!

Here's to your next **BULLSEYE!**

1,440
Your Daily Gift!

Each day blesses you with 24 hours. That's 1,440 minutes. No more. No less. Time is relentless. It can't be replaced or reversed. Stopped. Stored. Or saved. Nor can you reach into your time reservoir to "borrow" an hour from yesterday to use today.

Time is the essence of your life. If you waste your time, you waste your life.

Don't race compulsively to erratically do more "stuff" in less time. Don't become busier or more active. Instead, make better choices and wiser decisions. Then time becomes your ally, your valuable partner.

Don't confuse activity with results. You're not compensated for intent. You're paid only for results.

Steal time from the insignificant. Then channel it and your energies toward the significant—your goal, objective or anticipated result.

On the "clock of life" or "watch of winners," the key word is NOW! Procrastination is your foe. Indecision an assassin. Plan tomorrow tonight. Stay on track. Make every day count.

When you master your time, you master your destiny.

Bullseye Breakthroughs & Boosters:

- What one thing, could you do once a day...or one more time a day that would have a significant impact on your life or business?
- Let's imagine we walk out together, into the future for _____ years. (Please add your own timeframe.) When you look back at that time, what would you have liked to accomplish?
- How might time become your enemy...if you choose to do nothing?

A Taste of Cuban

Memorable Maverick!

Daily, I'm never quite sure where I'll discover that valuable nugget or significant keeper. That's why I always keep my eyes and ears open for "moments of significance." Here's an example.

I was in Dallas, conducting results-sessions for some of the top financial advisors in the world. The night before I spoke, I attended a reception and dinner, where the featured guest speaker was Dallas Mavericks owner Mark Cuban.

Cuban is a self-made billionaire. Before he bought the Mavericks in 2000 and became an NBA team owner, he made a boatload of money by founding two companies, Micro Solutions and broadcast.com, which he sold to yahoo.

Now I've seen Cuban interviewed lots. He's a frequent guest on sports broadcasts and has been featured and profiled in numerous newscasts. Plus, he's a celebrity investor on ABC's hit TV-show, *Shark Tank*.

As one of my radio producers used to say, Cuban "gives good air!" Meaning he fills the airwaves with entertaining anecdotes, quotes and opinions.

Cuban's detractors would say he's brash, arrogant and cocky.

Yet after hearing him speak (really answer questions for seventy-five minutes) and chatting with him briefly, I also found Cuban to be extremely likable.

Dressed in blue jeans and a baggy white shirt, Cuban sat comfortably in a director's chair on a stage, answering questions and sharing stories about his humble beginnings, work ethic, customer commitment, charitable donations, player negotiations and new business ventures.

He was direct. Smart. Funny. Honest. Entertaining. And memorable. Being memorable, is something Cuban especially values. Here's why.

When he was asked, "What's your goal for your team/franchise?", he replied with what I'll label as an unrehearsed burst of brilliance:

> "My business really isn't about basketball or for that matter, winning games. My purpose is to create memories, so fans will forever remember their experience at a Mavs game. The next day, I want their throats to still be raw from screaming. Their hands, still red from clapping. And their feet, still sore from stomping."

That's brilliant!

Cuban is singularly focused on the outcomes, results, benefits, advantages, value and memories his "product" produces.

Of course, he knows the importance of winning, yet it must be in a unique and memorable environment. One that's unforgettable. One that generates positive word-of-mouth. One that helps sell over 17,000 seats per game.

Cuban knows memories drive revenue. To best create those indelible mind impressions, Cuban is an active participant. He can be seen cheering his players and screaming at refs from the sidelines. Or cueing the audio engineer at a Mavs game to pump up the volume. He knows music that's loud, thumping and stirring revs-up the crowd.

Cuban is also easily accessible. Daily, he answers hundreds of e-mails from fans. He knows this type of "personal relationship" with customers also creates the right memories.

Bullseye Breakthroughs & Boosters:

- What memories are you creating for your customers?
- What's the "purpose" of your business?
- How do you communicate with your customers? How often?
- What type of "word-of-mouth" messages are being said and spread about you and your business?

Raise Your Ceiling
Daddy, when do we hit...?

What will drive you to new heights of success? Is it altruism or capitalism? Is it what you can give or what you can get? Is it selflessness or selfishness? Where will your journey take you?

Several years ago, en route on a flight to New Zealand, the man sitting next to me was Al Wilkerson. Al told me a story that happened to him with his three-year-old daughter Alycia, when she was flying for the first time.

As the 747 rolled down the runway, Alycia had a look of fascination and joy. But as the plane started to climb, her face became filled with fear and panic. She kept looking up and then to him, up and at him...until she finally shouted, "Daddy, when do we hit the ceiling?"

Remember, there are no ceilings, no parameters, no boundaries—unless *you* put them there. And when you're breaking through your own mental boundaries, it's not trespassing.

BULLSEYE!

One of my clients actually placed an eight-inch by eight-inch ceiling tile on the desk of every employee in his company. Emblazoned on each are these words:

Raise your ceiling!

Bullseye Breakthroughs & Boosters:

- What mental boundaries to your success, have you created?
- How will you overcome them and raise your ceiling?
- Have you allowed others, to create artificial parameters or barriers to your success?
- How will you remove them?

My Favorite Redhead
You Never Forget Your First.

To gaze into the future often requires a brief peek into the past.

And I see before me a little boy. A little boy who at the age of six stands in his first-grade classroom. He's asked by his teacher, Miss Northrup, to pronounce two words: "listen" and "rabbit."

The little boy, confidently and proudly exclaims, "Wis-sin and wabbit!"—and ev-wee-buddy waffs. So he repeats the words again, more loudly this time. Once more he says, "Wis-sin and wabbit!" And this time, ev-wee-buddy waffs even woud-uhr and wong-uhr.

The little boy goes home, tired, depressed and frustrated. He says to his pehr-ints, "My teach-uh, Miss Nawth-wup is cwazy, she cwaims I need speech caw-weckshun wessons. Can you bih-weeve that? She's wong. I can too pwo-nounce my ahs and ehls, just wis-sin."

Every day, that little boy works very hard on correctly pronouncing his Rs and Ls. Until finally, one day, after three years of speech correction lessons, he's able to enunciate, articulate and communicate. And I assure you, I know that little guy, real, real well!

Eventually, he grew-up to become a Hall of Fame speaker, a bestselling author, an attorney, and a wadio and teh-wuh-vision talk-show host!

Yep, I'm that little boy! At the age of six, (unbeknownst to me at the time), my life and career choice were being shaped and influenced. I've often wondered, what my life would be like if I had properly pronounced "listen" and "rabbit." (Maybe I'd have played shortstop, batted third and led the Cubs to a World Series championship? Okay, maybe not!)

The reason I share one of my childhood experiences with you is because it's a story about a journey. A journey of results. Confucius said, "Every great journey begins with a single step."

And those steps aren't always sure and steady. Often, there are stumbles. Missteps. Or even falls. Yet the key is to dust yourself off. To rise. And to give it another shot.

Those shots and attempts are significantly easier, when you have folks who believe in you, standing at your side. Encouraging you. Urging you to reach your potential. To stretch yourself.

In my life, I've been incredibly blessed to have lots of encouragers and mentors, who pushed, prodded and pulled me to excel. And one of my earliest was my first-grade teacher, Donna Northrup.

Even at the age of six, I knew Donna was a knockout! A stunning redhead. Yet most important, she believed in me. She knew I could convert ridicule to results. An impediment to talent.

Over the years, Donna and I stayed in touch. Yet the first time as an "adult" that I saw her, was in the summer of 2000 at a party. It was there, I gave her a copy of one of my books, *Peak Your Profits*. She thanked me. Hugged me. And cried.

Then, in January of 2004, I sent Donna a copy of one of my other books, *Stop Whining! Start Selling!* In the *Special thanks to* section, I wrote:

> Donna Northrup...
>
> My first-grade teacher, who didn't laugh when she first heard me speak. Instead, she cheerfully encouraged me to attend my daily speech cuh-weck-shun wessons. Little did she realize she was shaping my life and career.

Then, in February of 2004, I got a call from Donna. She asked, "What are you doing on June second?" "I'm in-town," I said. "Why?"

"Since you're a Chicago Cub nut like me," she said, enthusiasm filling her voice, "How'd you like to go to a Cubs game and sit right behind the visitor's dugout?"

"Cool!" I exclaimed. "Do I have to turn in any missing assignments from 1963?" She laughed and said, "Be ready at 11:00, I'll pick you up in a limo."

June 2, 2004 was one of the most memorable days of my life. It was almost surreal to realize, I was cheering on my beloved Cubbies with my first-grade teacher!

At holiday time, Donna and I would always chat. Catch-up. And reminisce. She was always interested. Always encouraging. Always teaching.

Then, in October of 2006, Donna was diagnosed with a malignant brain tumor. I was devastated. As were her friends, family and thirty-three-years-worth of other first grade students.

But when we chatted, she was optimistic, although accepting of her plight. She asked, "Jeff, do you think you can see your first-grade teacher one more time?"

On a crisp, Sunday afternoon in November I visited Donna at her home.

When she greeted me at the door with the help of a friend and her niece, I gave her a bouquet of red roses. The card read, "Red roses for my favorite redhead!"

Her face lit up as she motioned me toward her kitchen table. We chatted for about thirty minutes. What I remember, is we held hands. We laughed. We began most sentences with, "Do you remember the time that...?" Or, "Whatever happened to...?"

Yet, what I especially remember, is the kitchen clock ticking...loudly. With each tick, it erased another second.

Donna said, "Jeff, I'm tired, but I'm so glad you came. She slowly walked me to the door. We embraced and both stated simultaneously, "I love you!"

I just wanted Donna to know I was thinking of her. So we spoke again before Thanksgiving, Christmas and New Year's Eve in 2006. With each conversation, she was alert, but her voice grew softer. Weaker.

Then, sadly, on January 7, 2007, my favorite redhead began "teaching" from a new classroom. Located not in Lincolnwood, Illinois, but a far loftier place.

She will forever be missed, but never forgotten.

Henry David Thoreau, once said,

> "It is something to be able to paint a particular picture, or to carve a statue, and so to make a few objects beautiful; but it is far more glorious to carve and paint the very atmosphere and medium through which we look. To affect the quality of the day - that is the highest of arts."

Donna Northrup Duffy profoundly affected the quality of my day and the quality of my life. For these gifts, I'm forever grateful.

So:

> Whose "day" will you affect?
>
> Who has affected your "days?"
>
> Have you said, "Thank you."?
>
> Have you told them, "I love you!"?

If not now, then when? For remember, the clock is ticking.

Bullseye Breakthroughs & Boosters:

- Who has made a significant impact on your life—personally or professionally? How have you thanked them? A call? A note? An email?

BULLSEYE!

When will you thank them—again—or for the first time?

- How can *you*, make a difference in someone else's life: A family member? A friend? A teammate?
- How will you acknowledge, that time is one of your most valuable assets? And your clock, is always ticking.

A Champion's Vision
Winning Wingspan.

In the Spring of 2000, I consulted with Bill Russell—considered by many to be the most celebrated athlete in the history of sports. His feats of victory read more like a "believe it or not" tale rather than a resume of remarkable results.

His accomplishments included:

- 11 NBA World Championships in 13 seasons with the Boston Celtics
- NBA Hall-of-Famer
- The only athlete to ever win two NBA Championships as a player/coach
- Voted one of the top 50 NBA players of all time
- Two NCAA Championships with the University of San Francisco
- Olympic Gold Medal Winner
- Recognized by HBO as the greatest winner of the 20th century

One of the most interesting stories Russell told me was about his role as a rebounder.

He turned rebounding into a science!

Russell did more than merely elevate his angular 6'10" body to grab the ball or "wipe the glass" following an opponent's errant shot. Instead, he turned rebounding into a science.

Russell studied other players. He learned their tendencies. Their shot-patterns. Their habits. Especially the bad ones. This analysis gave him an almost unfair competitive advantage. When an opponent launched a shot, other players followed the ball. Not Russell.

Instead, he fought for a position in more valuable territory. He was headed to where the ball was going after it hit the backboard or rim on a missed shot.

This strategy, dogged determination, and exhaustive preparation helped Russell become the most prolific rebounder of his time. (He averaged 22.5 per game and led the league in rebounding four times.)

Get rid of it. Fast!

But Russell knew once he had the ball, he had to get rid of it. Fast!

His next goal: quickly fling the ball downcourt via an outlet pass to a streaking teammate. With speed and precision, Russell would grab a rebound and hurl a pass up the hardwood.

He wasn't throwing to a teammate as much as he was throwing to a spot. A spot a teammate would suddenly fill so that he could dribble to the bucket or pass to another teammate—the result: two more fast-break Celtic points.

Throughout a game, Russell would toss a lot of so-called "no look or blind passes." He told me the "blind" pass is a misnomer because "Tossing the ball to a player you can't see, is dumb!" And Russell wasn't dumb.

When I asked how he perfected the "outlet" pass, he rose before me, extended his long arms in front of his body, spread the fingers on his enormous hands and said, "I worked on and improved my peripheral vision. Every day, I'd slowly extend each hand. A little to the left. A little to the right."

Eventually, his hands, though extended at his sides like a bird's awesome wingspan, were still in his line of sight. Just like the court. Just like a streaking open teammate, who would take Russell's bullet pass in full stride and head for the hoop.

"Clear peripheral vision, gives you focus," Russell said. "You have to rid yourself of peripheral opponents."

Bullseye Breakthroughs & Boosters:

- Keep your eyes open for opportunity.
- Results require teamwork and time.
- Prepare for victory.
- Work smart, every day. Focus.
- Avoid distractions or "peripheral opponents."
- Develop your strengths.
- See what others don't see, then take action.

BULLSEYE!

(On July 31, 2022, Bill Russell died at the age of 88. On August 11, 2022, the National Basketball Association announced, to honor the life and legacy of Russell, his jersey No. 6 would be retired across the entire NBA. Russell joins baseball's Jackie Robinson (No. 42) and hockey's Wayne Getzky (No. 99), as the only professional athletes in United States sports history to have their jersey numbers retired league-wide.)

Seinfeld Says

What's the deal with…?

When I was hosting my radio talk-show on Chicago's WFYR, I was preparing to leave our studios, when my executive producer asked, "Where you headed?"

I answered, "To tape an interview with a young comedian."

"Any good?" she wondered.

"Very funny," I told her. "Very talented."

"What's his name?"

"Jerry Seinfeld."

"Never heard of him," she said.

My time with Jerry was memorable. He was funny, yet also laid back and gracious, a terrific guest.

While this was before his iconic TV show, what I especially remember, is Jerry's classic query about things that baffled him. He'd ask, "What's the deal with…?"

Those four words, have actually been instrumental, as I work with and coach clients. Especially, when it comes to honoring commitments. Clients always request I hold them "accountable" or "hold their feet to the fire."

Yet, that only happens, when folks do what they say they're going to do.

If a client tells me, "I'm going to do that."—they know I'll ask, "By when?" It's the execution of, "I'll do X by Y." And if they don't...

They know I'll politely inquire, "On (date), you told me, you'd do blank-by-blank. That didn't happen. As Jerry Seinfeld might say, 'What's the deal with that?'" And they're grateful, I kept 'em accountable.

Bullseye Breakthroughs & Boosters:

- How do you keep YOU accountable? How 'bout others?
- How can you repeatedly apply the success formula of "I'll do X by Y." It simply answers, "what" you'll do and by "when".
- How successful are you at honoring your commitments?
- How can you improve?

Erase or Embrace
Always relevant and timeless.

I first wrote the following in 2001, after 9/11. Over the past two-plus decades, I've shared it in keynotes, results-sessions, newspaper columns and interviews. And folks tell me, "Jeff, its message is always relevant and timeless."

May it too, help you like it has helped others—to embrace your future with hope vs. hesitancy.

Erase villains. Embrace heroes.

Erase reluctance. Embrace resilience.

Erase selfishness. Embrace selflessness.

Erase getting. Embrace giving.

Erase complaining. Embrace changing.

Erase observing. Embrace doing.

Erase negatives. Embrace positives.

Erase mere interactions. Embrace meaningful relationships.

Erase boundaries. Embrace possibilities.

BULLSEYE!

Erase delay. Embrace now.

Bullseye Breakthroughs & Boosters:

- What are the "things" in your life that you oughta erase?
- What are the "things" in your life that you oughta embrace?
- When will you take action?

Jenner's Journey
Don't Know Caitlyn. Did Know Bruce.

Bruce Jenner walked into our radio station early. He had a big smile, a warm handshake and a friendly, relaxed demeanor. Bruce was gracious, charming and funny. On-the-air and off.

Some guests would only be "on" when the red light was on. Not Jenner. He conveyed the message, "I'm happy to be here!" And following our interview, he even hung around to pose for pictures with me and other members of the WFYR radio team.

It was the 1980s, long before the relentlessly-hyped, headline-grabbing April 24, 2015 conversation between Jenner and ABC's Diane Sawyer, seen by 17 million viewers. While frequently promoted as *The Interview*, there was a far more valuable and impactful Bruce Jenner dialogue to me.

My interview with him, when Jenner was a guest on my radio talk-show in Chicago, *The Connection*.

When Jenner and I visited, he wasn't a "reality TV star." In reality though, he was a star. A big one. A celebrity. An Olympic gold medalist. An American hero!

Our focus here won't be on Jenner's transgender announcement. Instead, it'll be on our conversation over thirty-five years ago. What I learned from him then and have applied for four decades. And what you too can learn from him and apply with remarkable results. If you choose.

Yet there's one thing Jenner said during the ABC commercials to promote his interview with Sawyer, I found especially interesting. Because when I heard it, it immediately took me back to *our* interview.

Jenner said in the ABC TV spots, "My whole life has been getting me ready for this." And I realized, that's quintessential Jenner. Really no different "today" versus decades ago, with his approach or preparation.

For what I learned then about Bruce Jenner is...

He's a focused, disciplined winner. Jenner knew how to prepare mentally and physically for victory. How to become a world-record-holder and a gold medalist in the grueling Olympic decathlon competition.

As a radio and TV broadcaster, I interviewed many professional athletes who performed at peak or championship levels. And all of them had one thing in common. They visualized their success. Visualization helped them create a mental rehearsal for the real thing.

Yet the most striking example of the power of visualization, is Jenner's. I asked Bruce to tell me about his gold medal and record-setting decathlon victory in Montreal in 1976.

Bruce interrupted me and said, "Jeff, I didn't win the gold in '76, I won it in '72!" I said, "Excuse me?!" And he said, "Let me explain. Jeff you're right, technically I won the gold in 1976 in Montreal, but I really won it in 1972, when I lost in Munich."

He said the victory in Montreal was for the world to witness, but what he called the "victory in '72," was even harder to secure, because it was a victory only within his mind.

He told me from the moment he lost in Munich in 1972, he began to rededicate and recommit himself to his goal, the gold medal in the decathlon.

He saw himself victorious every day for the next four years. He saw himself standing on the victor's platform with the gold medal draped around his neck. He saw himself circling Olympic Stadium waving the American flag. Bruce Jenner visualized victory and it became reality.

To see Jenner's story as told by me in an excerpt or "classic cut" from our *Vintage Video Vault* and my *How to Set and Really Achieve Your Goals* video, please go to this YouTube channel, *Jeff Blackman's ResultsTV* link:

LINK: https://tinyurl.com/BlackmanJennerGold

Bruce Jenner's success is a dramatic testament to the impact of visualization. And visualization is also linked to another step in positively programming your belief system.

And that's graphic reinforcement or using pictures to help you focus on your dream(s), desired outcome(s) or goal(s). Bruce Jenner also used this winning strategy.

Jenner told me he took a picture of the gold, silver and bronze medalists from the 1972 Olympic games and then altered the picture in a unique way.

He cut out from the picture, the head of the gold medalist. And in its place, he pasted his own face. For the next four years, he stared at a picture showing him, Bruce Jenner, to be the gold medalist.

He once again stressed, "Jeff, I won the gold in my mind and in that picture, after I lost in Munich in 1972." He added, "I merely went to Montreal in 1976, to pick up a medal I already won!" How's that for a powerful example?

What might your pictures or words of graphic reinforcement be? For your life? Career? Business? If you'd like, here's a fun project.

When I'm conducting goal setting results-sessions, I have participants create goal setting achievement posters or vision boards. They're surrounded by personal photos and lots of magazines.

The magazines are a source of inspiration—with articles, words, phrases, headlines and pictures about successful people or ads promoting products people might like to own, places they'd like to visit or experiences they'd like to have.

These images and words can be pasted on to the goals posters. One side or both sides. One poster or more. Within the poster's borders or beyond. No rules! No boundaries!

For I stress to folks, "When you're busting beyond your own mental boundaries, it's not called trespassing!"

Graphic reinforcement can be a single picture, or with the goals posters, it can be several pictures. The vision boards tell a story of accomplishment and success at both personal and professional levels.

Clients' posters have included pictures of their dream home, a vacation getaway, a new car, the corporate logo of a prospect they're pursuing, an ideal weight, or words reinforcing their lifestyle or approach to business, i.e., *family first, teamwork, persistence, healthy, innovation, imagine what's possible or We Can!*

Whatever your hopes, dreams and goals are...

See them.

Believe them.

Pursue them.

Realize them.

Yet always remember, goals are only realized with a process in place to seek and attain them. And we, as individuals and as a world progress, because we "see" and choose to have a better life.

Here's to:

   √ *Your* better life...

   √ *Your* better business...

   √ *Your* better you...

As you stand upon *your* victory stand!

Bullseye Breakthroughs & Boosters:

- Be true to yourself.
- Be gracious, friendly and courteous.
- Smile, make others feel comfortable.
- Determine how you will "get ready" for life.
- Be a positive optimist and envision or see your victories.
- Never accept or allow others' negativity to diminish your passion and purpose. There will always be predictors of doom and gloom, naysayers, detractors, judgmental critics—accept that—yet realize that your happiness, is about your happiness, NOT somebody else's.

Reach for the Moon

Lovell's Lore.

Goals turn fantasy into fact. Dreams into reality. Goals are the progressive movement toward, and eventual realization of...a worthwhile idea.

Specify your goals. Write them down. Set a target date. Take action.

In his inaugural address, President John Fitzgerald Kennedy declared, "By the end of the 1960s, an American astronaut would be on the moon." Many were disbelieving, but not Apollo 13 astronaut, Jim Lovell. He believed!

When Lovell was a guest on my TV talk-show, I asked him about Kennedy's goal. His response:

> "When we heard the objective, it was...can we do it? Kennedy said before the decade is out...that was about nine years away. It was a challenge, but we dug in and accomplished it. It's always healthy to set new goals. Don't look back, don't rest on your laurels or the past, it's what can you do now! It

requires an optimistic mindset. It requires you try new adventures."

Pursue new adventures. Set new goals. Reach for the moon!

To see an excerpt or "classic cut" from our *Vintage Video Vault* of my TV interview with Jim Lovell, please head to:

LINK: https://tinyurl.com/BlackmanLovell

Bullseye Breakthroughs & Boosters:

- A written goal is far better, than a faded memory.
- If you're going to make a bold declaration, in front of witnesses, you better get to work— and do it.
- A goal without a deliverable or target date, is simply a fantasy.
- What's your new adventure?

Madness with Meaning
A Winner's Mindset!

For basketball fans, there's no month better than March. Affectionately dubbed *March Madness*, it's a time with a seemingly endless string of basketball games; the NIT (National Invitational Tournament) for men's basketball, plus the *Big Dance* – the NCAA (National Collegiate Athletic Association's) tourneys for men and women. And as a bonus, there's your state high school tournaments for the boys and girls.

One can literally watch, hundreds of games. Did you cancel all appointments and tell folks you'll see 'em in April?!

While it's a time for school spirit, alumni support, community involvement and playing heroics, it's especially fun, when your team keeps winning, surviving, advancing!

Then—fans, journalists, coaches and broadcasters devote hours of discussion and debate to match-ups, playing styles, upset specials and bold predictions.

One of the best b-ball analyzers and prognosticators is Clark Kellogg. If you're a basketball fan, your immediate reaction is, "Yep, he's good!" If you're not, you'll soon still value his opinions and insights.

In the summer of 2005, Clark and I were speakers on the same program. That gave us the opportunity to chat about lots of stuff. Especially, winning.

That's a topic, Clark knows lots about. As an observer and a participant.

First, some quick background on Clark. He played his college ball at Ohio State. In 1982, he earned All-Big Ten and Most Valuable Player honors. He then became the Indiana Pacers number one draft pick. He was a unanimous selection to the 1982 NBA All-Rookie Team.

Clark only played five NBA seasons before retiring with chronic knee problems. He had career averages of 18.9 points and 9.6 rebounds per game.

As a broadcaster, he's in his thirtieth year as a basketball analyst for the CBS Television Network's NCAA Tournament coverage. And for 21 years, he was a TV analyst for the NBA's Indiana Pacers broadcasts.

So when it comes to winning, competition and preparation, it's fair to say, Clark is a reputable and credible expert!

The last time I saw him, was on February 25, 2012. It was about thirty minutes before tipoff at the University of Kansas' Allen Fieldhouse. It was the final time Kansas would meet Missouri, as a conference foe. (Mizzou is now in the SEC or Southeastern Conference.)

I was at the game with our eldest daughter Brittany, at that time, a Kansas senior and a rabid KU basketball fan.

I said, "Brit, that's Clark Kellogg." She asked, "How do you know?" I told her, "Six-foot, seven-inch guys are easy to spot and we know each other!"

As I bellowed-out, "Clark!" he stopped and greeted me with a warm handshake and big smile.

While our conversation that afternoon was brief, I never forgot what he shared with me years earlier. Here's a sampling of his wisdom:

Jeff Blackman: What do all winners have?

Clark Kellogg: Winning starts with an attitude. It's striving for excellence. Wanting to be good. Winners put in the time and energy. It's more than wins and losses, it's how you go about becoming better. It's a desire.

Winners must constantly prioritize. And that's a constant struggle. Because you have to ask yourself: What's important? Where will you invest your time? What will you sacrifice?

Winners know it's a juggling act. And it really never ends. I still wrestle daily with what I need to do vs. what I like to do. Where do I invest my resources?

In the mid to late 80s, you were running up and down the court with some of the greatest NBA players of all time, what was that like?

Going up against the Chicago Bulls' MJ (Michael Jordan) was phenomenal. He was so competitive. His will, skill and determination. When something was at stake, he rose, repeatedly. He took things personally between the lines. Yet his greatness elevated, when he learned to play as a teammate. That's when he really became a winner.

I also bumped heads with Charles Barkley. He had strength, tenacity and the will to make it happen.

However, the greatest winner I ever played with, was Herb Williams at Ohio State and with the Indiana Pacers. He really knew the game and played with energy and passion.

What lessons has basketball taught you about life?

Life's not always fair, but what you put in the wash, comes out in the rinse. We're not all blessed with the same gifts or resources. Yet when you don't win on the "scoreboard"—you may still win because you've done your very best. That's as immediate as it gets, even in defeat.

In 1979, in high school, I played for Cleveland's St. Joseph's Academy in the Ohio state championship game. We lost. At Ohio State University in 1980, my teammates and I battled Indiana for the Big Ten championship. We lost. Then, in 1982, we fought Minnesota for the conference crown. We lost again.

Yet, what I learned is when you compete for the top prize, you have to be ready, with integrity and passion. Then, you can do your best, know you did your best and realize, you may still come up short.

You see Jeff, winners are thought of, in a different light, for when you compete valiantly, there's self-respect and the respect of others.

Yet don't be burdened by expectations, focus on the opportunity to elevate your performance and your teammates. When you're a key cog, your responsibility goes beyond just being ready, i.e., when you're a high draft pick, others have confidence in your ability. Use that confidence, to deliver the right results.

Clark, if we head out to the hoop on my driveway, for a spirited game of HORSE, who would win?

Jeff, I think I could handle you!

(In 2010, Clark played President Barack Obama in a game of POTUS, *President of the United States*—and lost!)

Bullseye Breakthroughs & Boosters:

So what lessons has Clark taught us? There are many:

- Winning starts with a positive attitude.
- Execution must be preceded by planning and prioritization.
- Desire and passion must be converted into action.
- Pay close attention to your competitors, what can you learn.
- Pay close attention to your teammates, what can you learn and how can you help your team excel, so you all win.
- Study superstars and what makes them super.
- Acknowledge an individual's unique strengths and talents, yet know teams win championships and success is never a solo journey.
- Believe in yourself, confidence matters.

BULLSEYE!

- Be smart, keep moving with purpose and intention.
- Accept that on occasion, life ain't fair, stuff happens, you may lose, yet winners turn defeat into desire and turmoil to triumph.

So now, convert this message of March Magic into...

An Awesome April...

A Marvelous May...

A Jammin' June...

A...

Why? C.A.U.S.
Constant. Awesome.
Unduplicatable. Supremacy.

On a daily basis, I confronted the world's toughest negotiators.

No, not clients. My kids! Especially, when they were younger.

They were relentless. Aggressive. And didn't know the meaning of the word "No!"

To them, "no" simply set the stage for dialogue.

Therefore, I learned a powerful response to their constant queries of "Why?"

So when they asked, "Why?"—I became conditioned to exclaim, "Because!"

It was simple. Direct. And a momentary stop-gap.

However, "because" is two syllables and took too long to utter repeatedly.

Therefore, with extensive training, I developed the ability to answer the frequent "Why?" questions with only one syllable, "Caus."

BULLSEYE!

They asked, "Why?" I declared, "Caus!"

And I realized, wouldn't this be a robust retort to a prospect who wonders, "Why should we use you?" And all you needed to confidently respond with is "Caus!"

Here's what I mean.

What if "Caus" stood for:

Constant
Awesome
Unduplicatable
Supremacy

And that's exactly what *you* deliver! CAUS meaning:

Constant:

- on-going
- all-the-time
- non-stop

Awesome:

- phenomenal
- incredible
- extraordinary

Unduplicatable:

- can't be copied
- unique
- one-of-a-kind

Supremacy:

- highest quality
- superior
- the ultimate

When you offer the marketplace constant awesome unduplicatable supremacy...your customers benefit!

They tell the world. And you profit!

Here's a simple example of "CAUS" in action.

As you may know, here in Chicago, "the hot dog" is considered haute cuisine! And one of the best places to devour this Chicago tradition is at the Superdawg Drive-In.

Superdawg is a nostalgic throwback to the 1950s. Carhops attach a tray to your car window...that's stacked high with snap-when-you-bite-'em-Superdawgs™, hot and crispy Superfries™ and thick and rich Supershakes.™

And the Superdawg receipt boldly declares:

> "Our family has been thrilling customers with superfood and friendly service since 1948!"

Wow! How's *that* for a "CAUS" declaration!?

So when you're in Chicago and would like to witness and taste "constant, awesome, unduplicatable supremacy," ...call me!

Lunch is my treat!

Bullseye Breakthroughs & Boosters:

- Where can you deliver constant, awesome, unduplicatable supremacy in your life or business?
- What will you do, to be meaningful and memorable?
- How will you create loyal fans and enthusiastic zealots?

A Cup of Gratitude
Coffee Keeper.

Starbucks gets it!

Even if a "Thank you" was already uttered by a barista, the cup lid sticker stating "Thank you" reinforced the importance of gratitude.

Yet, how come so many folks, in business and life— forget the significance of a "Thank you" and the value of courtesy and respect?

Words like:

"Thank you"

"Please" and

"You're welcome."

Are never old-school, trendy or toss-away drivel. They are essential in how we interact, co-exist, live, and work with others.

What do you think?

Oh, by the way, THANK YOU for investing in *BULLSEYE!*, I'm grateful.

Bullseye Breakthroughs & Boosters:

- Being thankful, courteous, and respectful— are winning ways.
- Develop an attitude of gratitude.
- Kindness and class should never take a vacation.

Woodstock with Warren

The Oracle of Omaha.

The "journey" was hatched in the fall of 2017. It began with a simple question, "What if..." And boom, the four of us quickly exclaimed, "We're all in!"

The trek for my wife Sheryl, brother-in-law Bob, and sister-in-law Char, began on Friday, May 4, 2018. We flew from Chicago to Des Moines, Iowa. Then drove to Omaha, Nebraska.

What would inspire us to fly, drive and immerse ourselves in a weekend adventure? A rock concert? A family reunion? An unforgettable entertainment experience? The answers to all of the preceding, are an unequivocal, "Yes!"

We were official attendees of what the media dubbed *Woodstock for Capitalists!* As Berkshire Hathaway shareholders, we had the benefits and perks of attending their annual three-day shareholders' meeting.

The BH portfolio is vast and diversified. Whether you seek a tasty custard blizzard, delectable chocolates, a-snap-when-you-bite-'em-hot dog or secure insurance protection. As a holding company, BH's "holdings" include; Dairy Queen, See's Candies, Oscar Mayer and GEICO.

These holdings, plus others, along with their huge portfolio of other companies' stocks, makes Berkshire Hathaway, by market capitalization, the sixth largest company in the world.

And its founder, chairman and CEO, Warren Buffett, is the world's third-wealthiest person, who has the iconic "title" of: *The Oracle of Omaha!* (Buffett's net worth in 2022, an astonishing: $97 billion.)

The "BH" or "Berky experience" was attended by approximately 40,000 people, who flocked to Omaha. Where during "shopping days" you can buy at a "savings" products and services from booths that comprise the BH portfolio. (Notice, I said at a, "savings." In the 2017 shareholder letter, Buffett actually declared, "Your Chairman discourages freebies.")

Twenty-thousand "capitalists" or fans or zealots, also crowded into Omaha's CenturyLink Center for the full-day, Saturday, May 5 meeting. (In 2017, the meeting's live stream was watched by 3.1 million viewers. And replays with shorter meeting excerpts had 17.1 million views.)

The highlight of the meeting: Warren Buffett and his longtime friend, partner and BH vice chairman Charlie Munger, simply sat at a table on a CenturyLink Center stage and were peppered with questions. Two-and-a-half hours in the morning, and two-and-a-half hours in the afternoon.

For five hours, they fielded queries from journalists, analysts and worldwide shareholders. No notes. And no knowledge of what would be asked. Questions and answers covered: investment philosophy, succession planning, tariffs, ethics, cyber-attacks, Elon Musk, presidential politics, the newspaper business, culture, cryptocurrency, women in the workforce, and more.

In 2018, Buffet was 87. And Munger, who was 94, had a net worth of $1.64 billion. They're both smart. Really smart! Plus, they're articulate, poignant, relevant, insightful and remarkably funny! And they personify the significance and importance of "listening to your elders."

Buffett and Munger Wisdom

Charlie Munger: "You must always work to improve your judgment."

Warren Buffett: "What counts is having a philosophy and following a consistent plan."

Charlie Munger: "If you're going to live a long time, you have to keep learning."

Charlie Munger: "I've been to Google headquarters, it looked like a kindergarten." (Warren Buffett added: "A very rich kindergarten!")

Bullseye Breakthroughs & Boosters:

- Ethics, honesty, and doing the right thing are non-negotiables.
- Dream big.
- Hire bright people with specific skills...then get out of their way.

BULLSEYE!

- Be a lifetime student. (Buffett READS six hours a day.)
- Protect your reputation.
- Success takes time, discipline, and patience.
- Define what matters most in life for YOU, and know, that it shouldn't be money.
- When you invest, buy what you understand.
- Be wise, not greedy.
- Know when to take action, know when to wait.
- Price is what you pay—value is what you get.
- Do what you love.
- Give back as often as possible.
- Simple and easy is always better than complex and confusing.
- The best investment you can make is the investment in yourself.

Resolution Reality
Simplicity Works.

So at the end of a year—and the start of another—do resolutions work?

Hop online. Turn on the TV. Crank up the radio. Open the newspaper.

Print ads, broadcast commercials, and online messages urge you to:

"Lose weight!"

"Get in shape!"

"Eat healthy!"

"Change your life!"

So you can "Take advantage of incredible savings!" (Especially at the start of a new year.) And, to do it "Now!"

Diet and nutrition centers, fitness facilities, and weight reduction products are in an aggressive push every January for customer acquisition.

However, they needn't worry about customer satisfaction and retention. Why? Because most of these new customers ain't gonna be customers in a few weeks.

Oh, don't get me wrong. They won't be angry, frustrated, or disappointed customers. Instead, they'll be part of the January juggernaut, February Fade, or March madness that simply quits. Gives up. Waves the white flag. Surrenders. Not to some external force, but themselves.

Some might call this "customer churn" or attrition. It's not. Savvy retailers, businesspeople, and marketers know what it is. It's called "profit margin!"

But the real question is, "How come?"

Why do so many people start with good intentions to accomplish a defined goal yet get sidetracked? Why do they abandon their hopes, dreams and desires? How come they fall prey to obstacles?

Simple questions, but not always easy answers.

That's why resolutions seldom work.

Resolutions usually urge you to; avoid, delete, eliminate or reduce. Or to "add" something to your daily regimen that's new, untested, or unproven.

Neither the addition nor the deletion brings initially, great joy or happiness. Instead, it can be accompanied by pain, frustration, sweat and tears.

Ouch! Not much fun.

Success takes time. No magic bullets. No quick fixes. No special elixirs.

I once heard an NBC *Today Show* broadcaster ask Phil McGraw, Ph.D., a.k.a. *Dr. Phil*, "Do you believe in resolutions?" He quickly answered, "No. But I do believe in committing to projects with deadlines."

I agree. Here, simplicity works.

Dr. Phil also said, "At the end of the game, it's about results. Life is a full-contact sport and there's a score up on the board."

Bullseye Breakthroughs & Boosters:

- First, define the "what." What do you want to accomplish?
- Then, define the "when." What's the deadline, deliverable or due date?
- Next, determine the "how." What must you do?

A-to-Z, Be the Best You Can Be

Alphabet Soup of Success.

One of the great joys of being in my business, is that I get to do research everywhere—while visiting at a client's office, traveling on-the-road, surfing the Internet or even simply reading the Sunday newspaper.

And I once discovered a gem in Abigail Van Buren's column, *Dear Abby,* in the *Chicago Tribune.* It was called *To Achieve Your Dreams, Remember Your ABCs* by Wanda Hope Carter. It featured an A-to-Z listing of simple thoughts to pursue your dreams.

And it inspired me, to create a new A-to-Z listing of motivational messages—to help you achieve happiness, success and results in your business and life.

Here's my:

A-to-Z, Be the Best You Can Be!

Attitude and action drive your results.

Belief and behavior are a powerful combination.

Confidence helps pave your path to prosperity.

BULLSEYE!

Defeat is part of life. Learn from it.

Enthusiasm creates opportunity and results.

Focus on your goals and priorities. Avoid distractions.

Go for it!

Hope may not be a strategy, but it's sure a meaningful motivator.

"I did!"—is far better than, "I'll try."

Jump at the opportunity to help, to volunteer, to say, "I can do that!"

Knowledge creates growth. But remember, it isn't what you know, it's what you *do*, with what you know.

Love and laugh. Often!

Money matters. It gives you choice, freedom, and flexibility.

Navigate life's journey through the successes and the setbacks. It'll make you stronger.

Opportunity is always knocking. Be ready to answer.

Persistence and positivity are often the difference between winning and losing.

Quick isn't always the best solution. Patience pays.

Respect others. Be kind, courteous, and gracious.

Success and happiness are yours to pursue and achieve. Make it happen!

Truth is your friend. It doesn't require a good memory.

Unique is who you are. Embrace it. Share it!

A-to-Z, Be the Best You Can Be

Value your self-worth. If you don't, nobody else will.

Words matter. They can help or hurt. Choose wisely.

Xamine where you're at. Where you'd like to be. And how you want to get there.

You make a difference. Expect great things in your future.

Z isn't the end. It's a fresh start. Be the best you can be, living A-to-Z!

Time-Tested Truisms
Principles and Purpose.

When it comes to life and business, I've discovered time-tested truisms that are...

Bullseye Breakthroughs & Boosters:

- No matter how much you urge, cajole, educate and incent—if somebody doesn't want to do it faster, better or smarter, they ain't gonna do it. Or they'll half-heartedly attempt to do it, and justify why it didn't work! People only change for their reasons, motivations and desires.
- So first, understand others. Then, to help them succeed—define positive expectations, desired outcomes and a game plan for growth. Complemented by encouragement and accountability.
- Before you try to change the world, upgrade yourself. Start with your skills, attitudes and behaviors.

- Surround yourself with smart people. They can always give you a viewpoint that's fresh, honest and direct. (Remember, if two people are *always* in agreement, one of them ain't necessary!)
- Move forward. It's okay to reflect on the past, yet don't brood over it. If it didn't work, learn from it. Then: G.O.I.M.O. (*Get Over It, Move On!*)
- Analyze what was—to create your next—what will be.
- Add laughter and amusement to your day, i.e., take out an old picture of yourself, then ask yourself, "What was I thinking?!"
- Live a life of when, not if.

Life: A Series of Adjustments

Catch with Papa.

In 2019, my "birthday week" was unlike any other. The day before my 63rd birthday, February 19, my beloved 91-year-old dad, Irv, passed away. The day after my birthday, February 21, were dad's funeral and interment.

Dad was the best mentor a little boy or adult son could ever have.

He taught me the significance of little things that matter. He helped me understand grandiose plans are nice, but results inform the world. He stressed, "good work" brings success, but "great work" helps you achieve beyond your wildest expectations.

Dad taught me integrity is a non-negotiable. Do the right thing. Know life is a game, *AND* to get good at it, bust your butt, play by the rules. But that doesn't mean you can't be a creative, bold, independent thinker.

Dad was one of the smartest guys I knew. Yet he was baffled by a multi-line house phone, VCR, DVD player, fax machine and cellphone.

BULLSEYE!

To the world, he was a CPA, lawyer, board member, bank chairman or advisor. To me, he was, *Dad. Popp. Papa.* Or *Irv.* Terms of endearment, affection and love.

Dad had three great "loves"—his family, his work and food! (Am convinced, when we took a final peek at him in the coffin, running down his lips and chin was a small streak of barbeque sauce!)

Together, Dad and I "played hard." We spent many hours tossing a football, playing catch with a softball or baseball, taking batting practice, shooting baskets, firing hockey pucks, and turning any "ball-like" object, like a fruit or a vegetable, into a quickly flung projectile! (To mom's shock and "anger" because these activities were conducted *inside* the house!)

Following dad's death, the outpouring of love and admiration from across the world for him has been overwhelming. Folks repeatedly told my family and me about the difference dad made in their lives or careers.

One of the most profound things dad ever told me was, "JB, life is a series of adjustments."

And one of the ways we "adjusted"—was with sports, playing and watching them. Dad loved to play and watch sports. Me too. It was one of our shared passions.

It began when I was a little boy and Dad was in his thirties. I'd watch him play softball with his buddies on Sundays at Proesel Park in Lincolnwood. (A northern suburb of Chicago where mom and dad lived for 51 years.)

It's the community/area where I grew up and played competitive baseball from the age of six through high

58

school, where the guys I played with at Niles West won state championships.

Then, like Dad, my softball career began at nineteen and ended at fifty-two. (The exact age Dad stopped playing.) We even played together on his accounting firm's softball team. Dad, 52, was behind the plate. Me, 23, at shortstop.

Plus, a 16-inch softball always "traveled" with dad. (I brought one to every rehab facility he was in, following multiple surgical procedures or numerous visits to the Emergency Room.) I made sure of it.

When Dad entered a long-term care facility on May 10th, 2018, I again placed a softball in his room.

On February 19th, seven hours after Dad's death, my wife Sheryl and I removed Dad's belongings from his room. And securely tucked into one of the nightstand drawers, next to Dad's bed, was the 16-inch softball. I took it. Not knowing what to do with it.

Then, on my birthday, February 20, it hit me. I took a black Sharpie and scrawled:

Papa—For Our Eternal Game of Catch!

Love, JB

The next day at the funeral, other family members scrawled on the ball their personal messages. Yet, we don't have the ball. Dad does. It's inside the casket. Dad is clutching it. In his right hand.

Dad, I love you!

Now, we must adjust to life without my dad, Irv Blackman. Yet he'll forever live in our hearts, minds, and tummies. Yet it'll be different...

Because life is a series of adjustments.

Bullseye Breakthroughs & Boosters:

- Life is always in a state of flux, change and evolution.
- Life never returns to "the way it used to be" or "normal".
- How will you continually adjust?
- Treasure today. Be grateful for yesterday. Use your future, to forever remember your past.

Hang A Left at Shanksville

Life's Twists and Turns.

If you've heard me speak, you know I'll often pose to a group and each participant, three simple yet powerful questions, that I call the world's fastest-strategic plan:

1. Where are you?
2. Where would you like to be?
3. How would you like to get there?

The "reality" of these questions was driven home years ago. It was September 18, 2003.

My flight landed in Pittsburgh at 4:30 P.M. By 5:15, I was behind the wheel of my rental car. (By the way, how come when you rent a car, for the first sixty seconds you just sit there feeling stupid, trying to figure out how it works?!)

Before departing, I again glanced at the directions that would take me to Indian Lake, Pennsylvania. A trip I was told should take ninety minutes.

Confident and prepared, I pulled out from beneath the protective cover of the parking garage.

Immediately, I was greeted by the wrath, fury, and aftermath of Hurricane Isabel. A torrential rainstorm pounded the windshield. Fifty miles-per-hour winds shook the car.

Since I had been on the road for an exhaustive thirty seconds, I thought it would be an excellent time to pull over for a break!

Before I headed for the turnpike, I called the resort to ask them to tell my client I had landed and was on my way. And to confirm the directions a hotel employee had given me earlier in the week.

Patty answered the phone this time, saying, "Oh no, those directions are all wrong. Here's what you oughta do." She then gave me a new game plan.

With Patty's guidance, I attempted to reach the turnpike. But traffic was at a standstill. I called Patty again. She said, "Okay, change of plans."

That became a familiar and often repeated retort.

Patty's ongoing changes and suggestions would feature; a turnpike, highways, side roads, twisty paths, and blind curves. All being navigated in a downpour moving from left to right.

And her directions didn't always include street names or highway numbers. Instead, they began with, "Look for the sign that says Shanksville and hang a left." Or, "After you pass that funny-looking house on the right, get ready for a series of big bends."

Finally, after three hours, mission accomplished.

Patty greeted me with, "I've spent more time talking to you than all of my previous husbands!"

Bullseye Breakthroughs & Boosters:

- You might be wrong if you think you always know the best way to reach your destination. Consider alternatives.
- There's likely to be more than one way to "get there." Explore the possibilities.
- Seek the advice and counsel of those who genuinely know the strange twists and turns of an experience you're about to embark on. Use their knowledge to your advantage. Let them prepare you for the unexpected and potentially dangerous pitfalls. And how to safely avoid them.
- Know that requesting assistance is a sign of strength, not weakness.
- Pay close attention to the "signs." They alert you to what's ahead.
- Focus on what's in front of you.
- Appreciate that speed is essential. Yet it can also be dangerous. Also realize, that if you're going too fast, you'll miss the details, an alternative route or blow an opportunity. On occasion, slow and deliberate ain't bad.
- If you're headed for trouble, take corrective action. Fast!

Pedals with Purpose
Can We Do It? Yes, We Can!

The mountains rose before him. Majestic. Yet menacing. They could deliver delight or despair, hope or heartache.

However, he knew the real foe was not one of nature's great wonders. Instead, it was himself. Could he conquer the battle within his mind. The fatigue within his legs. The stress upon his machine. And not a machine that relied upon oil or gas for its power. Instead, it merely had two wheels. And its source of power was him.

But as he and the world would soon learn, he'd emerge victorious. A winner.

Okay, by now, you probably know whose tale I'm telling.

Likely, a winner of the *Tour de France* bike race. Right?

Wrong!

Instead, it's the story of PJ Harrigan. A client and friend.

BULLSEYE!

Several years ago, on August 11, 2001, PJ competed in the *Leadville Trail 100 Mountain Bike Race* in Leadville, Colorado. A 100-mile challenge affectionately called *The Race Across the Sky*.

To prepare for this grueling competition, PJ committed his mind and body.

Beginning in January 2001, PJ dedicated himself to a strict training schedule; no booze, no ice cream, a changed diet, limited coffee consumption and a new early-morning companion, a blaring alarm at 4:20 A.M.!

PJ would wake-up, hop on his bike and hit the pavement. Long before the hot, debilitating Phoenix sun would consume him. About 19 miles later, he'd shower and head to work.

With this exhaustive, yet dedicated strategy, by race day, PJ had lost 35 pounds.

(Hmm. Apparently, success requires dedication and sacrifice. A willingness to change. To do things differently. To tweak. Fine tune. And upgrade.)

PJ also invested in the right clothes. For he knew that Leadville is the highest city in the United States, looming 10,152 feet above sea-level. Plus, he'd be pedaling up, down and around five mountains. And through weather that would include sunshine, falling temps, rain, sleet, and hail.

(Do clothes make the person? Probably not. Yet they can sure protect you. Or offer security in a risky environment. Ah-ha! Taking control of your environment. That sounds like a good idea too.)

PJ also invested in a new bike. One light enough to climb yet still sturdy enough to absorb unforgiving and relentless punishment.

PJ told me he wanted a bike that would "Take the edge off the big bumps."

(Don't we all! Yet too often, we attempt to attack life's obstacles with "old equipment." We rationalize why the previous tools don't need to be upgraded. We refuse to invest energy, time, or money in things that would make our life easier. We forget the realization of a goal is just the accumulated acts of a series of intelligent choices, attitudes and behaviors.)

When I asked PJ how he prepared mentally, he told me that earlier in the year he and his crew chief pre-rode the course, so on race day "I wouldn't freak out."

They strategized about diet, times, locations, food, supplies, obstacles, what to wear, when to wear it, and even a special recovery drink.

(Apparently, success requires a game plan. Attention to detail. And an incredible commitment to preparation. For it's far easier to combat an obstacle you've already whupped in reality, or simply within your mind.)

The *Race Across the Sky* began with 700 hopeful bikers. Yet for many, their plan to pedal fell prey to pain. Only 67% finished. Plus, to be declared an official finisher, you had to complete this test of will and endurance, (through rain, sleet and hail), in under 13 hours.

And to earn the much-coveted Leadville belt-buckle, you had to finish in under 12 hours.

PJ was an official finisher. He was also a winner!

No, I didn't say he won the race. Instead, he won *his* race! For his goal, was to finish in under 12 hours. And he did. His official time, 11:58:37. Out of 422 finishers and 421 proud belt-buckle recipients, PJ was number 419. Wow! Well done!

(Set a goal. See it. Live it. Breathe it. Do it!)

The belt-buckle is on display in PJ's home.

(Recognition is a good thing. Trophies, medals, plaques, ribbons and even belt-buckles are cool! For they tell the world not about your grandiose plans, but instead, about your results.)

Bullseye Breakthroughs & Boosters:

When I asked PJ, what he learned about himself throughout this Leadville lesson, he told me:

You can always dig deeper:

- Do more than you think you can do.
- Focus on your goal and pursue it as if you've already realized it.
- Create a support system, like supportive family members or an encouraging coach.
- Give yourself positive self-talk, especially in turbulent times. For over the last 40 miles, PJ struggled with fatigue and an asthma attack, yet he refused to quit, constantly repeating a phrase from the *Bob the Builder* video series he watched with his kids, "Can we do it? Yes we can! Can we do it? Yes, we can!"

So what mountains will you conquer?

Pedals with Purpose

Can you do it?

Yes, YOU can!

Daddy Knows Best
My Dear Children.

I'm never quite sure where and when inspiration might hit me, like this letter I wrote on June 15th, 2008, *Father's Day*.

And while on Father's Day, dads traditionally *get* stuff, I got up early that 2008 morning, and wrote the following to *give* to my kids.

And whenever I re-read it, I realize there might be some meaty or meaningful messages for you, your loved ones, your peers, your business and the challenges and opportunities you're likely to encounter.

Welcome to the family!

* * * * *

June 15, 2008

My dear children: Chad, Brittany and Amanda:

While it's customary for *you* to give *me* something on *Father's Day*, I decided to give you something too.

BULLSEYE!

Years from now, you'll look back on this note and say "What the heck was he talking about?!"

So here's your list of *Daddy's Dynamic Dozen x 2*:

1. Let it be known I love you more than you'll ever know.
2. If I push or prod you on occasion, it's because I think you're capable of achieving so much.
3. When I ask you questions, it's really because I care about you, your life, your goals and your friends. Sorry if you think it's "annoying."
4. Read. A lot. Your life will be influenced significantly by the books you read.
5. Make new friends. Your life will be influenced significantly by the people you meet.
6. Ask yourself, "What would I do, if I knew it was impossible to fail?"
7. Know the value of observing and listening. You were given two eyes, and two ears, and only one mouth for a reason.
8. Work hard, at school and at your job. Remember, people are watching you. And making decisions about you. Is that fair? Don't matter. That's how the game is played.
9. Save your money. Invest in yourself.
10. Be kind, to yourself and others.
11. Truth is your friend.
12. Help your Mother.
13. Take action. If you want it, go for it. If you'd like it, ask for it.
14. Realize "rejection" and "no" are part of life. Get over it. Move on.
15. I will always love YOU. Although at times, I might not like your choices or behaviors. Yet I

know you'll learn from your mistakes. And choices. That's how you grow. Mature. And become even better and stronger than you are now.

16. You each are remarkable in your own way. Be nice to each other. Avoid name-calling. Never scare each other. Accept that, on occasion, family gets angry at family, yet find a way to work it out.

17. Never give another person permission to influence your mood, attitude or outlook on life. Those are your choices. Your responsibility.

18. Clean up after yourself. Put your clothes away. Make your bed. Don't leave dirty dishes in the sink. (It gets your Mom angry!)

19. Think BIG. Dream BIG. Place no limits on your life.

20. Find what makes YOU unique and special. Be passionate. Enjoy the adventure.

21. Hug those who are important to you. Tell them, "I love you!"

22. Don't gossip, spread rumors, or say negative things about others. It often backfires and returns to bite you on the tush.

23. Don't bake in the sun! Do take great care of your body. Exercise. Eat well! (Remember: "gum" isn't a food group!) Laugh. Laugh some more!

24. If any of the preceding is confusing or causes you to wonder, "Why is my dad so weird?"... simply go back, repeatedly, and re-read #1!

Beyond the Pomp and Circumstance
Reflect and Rejoice.

Larry Cassidy is a remarkable guy. Over the years, I've had the pleasure and privilege to work with Larry and four of his CEO or executive leadership groups in Orange County, California. At meetings, he sits at the head of the table. Observing. Listening. Paying close attention to detail.

When Larry speaks, his words are carefully chosen. They matter. A penetrating question. A wry comment. An impactful statement.

He challenges and inspires one to think. Ponder. Consider. Reconsider. And most important, take action. About their business. And their life.

We've had the opportunity to yak in-person, over-the-phone, via e-mail and in his happenin' convertible about lots of stuff; biz, life, baseball, attitude, space and even, commencement speeches.

Huh?

BULLSEYE!

Larry sent me something he had written on June 18, 2009. When I read it, I knew it deserved an even bigger audience. Thankfully, Larry agreed.

It packs a wallop.

Whether you're a recent college grad...

An upcoming college grad...

A young entrepreneur...

A veteran leader...

A savvy business pro...

Or a human being (of any age), trying to make a difference!

Here's Larry Cassidy's "commencement speech."

LIVE SO THE WORLD 'CRIES,' AND YOU REJOICE

"When you were born, you cried, and the world rejoiced, live your life so that when you die, the world weeps, and you rejoice." —a Cherokee saying

"When I told a friend that June would mark fifty years since graduating from college (from Miami University in southwest Ohio), he asked, 'Are you going back for your reunion?' I shook my head, 'No. Don't think I can swing it.'

He gave me a curious look, "Well, if you do go, any nuggets you'd pass on to the grads?" He smiled, adding, "Hard to believe it's been fifty years. It's so different now. I wonder if what we think would mean much to them?"

I thought about his questions. Etching 'wise' advice onto today's youth seems a seductive notion. And my friend was correct: changes over the last five decades have been seismic, affecting how we connect with others and live our lives.

Yet despite that, I believe the fundamentals for living a life of significance haven't budged. And we ignore at our peril those essentials which nourish relationships and create the foundation for a noble life.

We learn early that cutting corners exacts a stiff price. So why not pass on these hard-earned "lessons" as helpful advice?

There's good reason to pause: unasked advice from elders can land on the young as "preaching." Now in my eighth decade, I have yet to welcome gratuitous counsel or relish being told what to do.

So as I suggest the "blocking and tackling" that is essential to building a solid platform for your journey, I understand it's you who will make the final call.

On that note, I'll start with two comments:

First, congratulations! You persevered and earned your degree. Celebrate! You deserve it. Allow yourself a well-deserved pat on the back for a job well done. You now have evidence on your resume, you finish what you start.

Second, tall trees are anchored by strong roots. As are you. So be clear about who contributed to where you are today: parents, grandparents, teachers, coaches and counselors, to name but a few. Those who set the high standards, demanded commitment and urged you to reach higher and become more than you thought you could be. Take time to name them, find them and thank them.

Fifty years ago, I was a version of you: young, eager, hungry to test limits and excited to explore possibilities. Despite the uncertainty lying beyond your diploma, I urge you to consider that same quest.

Why?

Because what you see today will change tomorrow. The "doomsday scenario" — not finding a pay check or getting on with your career — will unwind. And you'll move forward to craft your life. As have the generations which preceded you.

So accept that neither timing nor luck picks favorites. You play the game with the hand you're dealt; For you it's to climb on the economic roller coaster at a time of epic concern—the world's financial system having been pounded by greed and excess.

As you do, you must decide how to navigate today's dicey circumstances, without the aid of previous experience or reliable "experts." No easy task, but you'll manage it, as did your predecessors.

And as you do, you'll build muscle required for the years ahead. Consider these your "butterfly" days: as the infant butterfly beats its fragile wings, pushing through its sturdy cocoon wall, it develops the strength to fly.

As you "beat your wings" to escape today's economic cocoon, you too will grow stronger. And in this process, you'll also encounter opportunity: how to best use this time to prepare for an even more demanding future, lessons that'll provide lasting value, and, how to seize the high ground that lies beyond your cocoon.

Years of study have equipped you with information, knowledge and technical skill, all important to success. Yet these assets, alone or enhanced with post-graduate work, are insufficient for a life of meaning and significance.

For that, you must define, then discard or develop, those capabilities which hinder or support you becoming the best version of yourself: first, behaviors to purge which hinder personal growth; and second, those to develop which provide a solid lifetime foundation.

In the early 1500s, Michelangelo sculpted the Biblical King David. When asked how he created such a perfect likeness of David from a raw block of marble, Michelangelo answered, "I chipped away the pieces of stone which were not David."

I ask you: What do you chip off your block?

Here are three "malpractices" I propose:

1. Lose the excuses and justifications. These are smoke screens deployed to justify oversight and unfulfilled commitment. Do not bite off more than you can chew. However, once you accept a task, "own" it and complete it as agreed.

Know also, in this complex world, good intentions and best-laid plans will go astray. Your choice is then one of character: do you deflect liability, or do you step up, own your failure, and put it right?

Choose carefully. These are the hard decisions which shape your reputation.

2. Do not wallow in yesterday or count on tomorrow. Lingering in the past or reliving previous setbacks will cost you valuable energy.

The importance of yesterday is written in what you apply today. Nor will expecting tomorrow to fix things play out any better. "Hoping" is not a strategy; and, tomorrow is forever a day away.

If you mean to achieve change and reach goals, focus your energy on today. Take action today. If you move the needle each day, be it an inch or a mile, you'll be in position on the next day to launch from higher ground.

3. Give up the need to be right. Whether seeking status, control or self-esteem, the need to be right extracts far too high a price: it chokes off new input and options and curbs the creative thinking vital to shaping better solutions.

Served up with emotional heat, the need to be right skewers relationships and erodes respect. Tame it or you will not be welcome in a team-oriented future.

Those are big stumbling blocks I suggest you discard.

Instead, embrace my proposed eight qualities or "beliefs" to help you, be the best you:

1. I BELIEVE WE DO BEST BY BEING OURSELVES.

You may fool others, but seldom for long; in time, both your "cover" and credibility will implode. The best choice is to be authentic. Always.

You come to this life with useful tools. Apply them and play to your strengths. It's upon strength, one builds success. So find the labor you love, a role you fancy, and a setting that works for you.

Then take your best shot. And remember: "You have but one tool: yourself. Everything else is just tricks." Stick with the real you. In the long run, nothing works better.

2. I BELIEVE IN BEING 'IN THE MOMENT.'

You now enter an arena in which execution and accountability are increasingly prized, where many savor the "action." However, constant action can become an aphrodisiac.

There's an alternative: being "in the moment," quiet, curious and aware, inviting rich questions and real answers to emerge.

You know what you know, and it's substantial. Yet it's what you do not know, the undiscovered nuggets, which often determine the outcome.

3. I BELIEVE IN DOING THE RIGHT THING, AND FOR THE RIGHT REASONS.

You've done enough living to understand what is and what is not right and why it is right. If it doesn't feel right, don't do it.

As Peter Marshall reminds us, "We know perfectly well what we ought to do, but there are times we just don't want to step up and do it." Sorry. Temptation is not justification.

Making the right move under pressure is about integrity, honor and character, described well by the Air Force Academy as "...those qualities of moral excellence that stimulate a person to do the right thing, to take the right and proper actions, despite internal or external pressures to the contrary."

If you commit to doing the right thing as your only option, regardless of cost, you'll find even once-difficult calls to be self-evident.

4. I BELIEVE IN LIVING WITH PURPOSE AND PASSION.

Joe E. Lewis said, "You only live once, but if you work it right, once is enough." Life is not a rehearsal. "Working life right" happens when you are clear about your purpose: that pursuit which captivates you, summons your enthusiasm, and calls you to commit yourself completely.

Find your purpose and invest it with all your passion. You'll accomplish nothing of great import without such purpose and passion.

5. I BELIEVE IN DOING OUR BEST AND BEING THE BEST WE CAN BE.

You cannot do more than your best. However, you do not have the right to give an assignment less than your best effort.

If you cannot commit fully, it's better you decline the task. However, treat it as a sacred trust once you accept an obligation. Others ride on your pledge.

6. I BELIEVE IN, DO NOT GIVE UP. EVER.

Since my treatment for cancer, I've kept poet John Dryden's battle cry atop my desk: "I am wounded, but I am not slain. I will lay me down to bleed awhile, then rise to fight again."

Expect to be deceived, knocked down, stricken, and to see your best efforts fall short. Put these disappointments behind you, and resolve that you will not quit.

There will be days when you have exhausted your intellect, talent and strength, and you fear you can no longer go on. You must rise and fight again.

It was such spirit which Hall of Fame football Coach Vince Lombardi most valued: "The difference between success and failure is not a lack of strength, nor a lack of knowledge, but rather a lack of will."

7. I BELIEVE IN THE POWER OF LOVE.

Robert Kennedy wrote, "Real love is something unselfish. It involves sacrifice and giving."

Mother Theresa described real love as empowering small moments: "What we need is to love without getting tired. If we love until it hurts, there will be no more hurt, only more love. In this life, we can do no great things, only small things with great love."

Be unselfish and giving. Do not permit love to tire. And endow the "small things" with great love.

8. I BELIEVE IN BELIEVING...

In oneself. In others. And in wisdom and power beyond human capacity. And I do so for good reason: life places hard choices and difficult obstacles along our road. We're equipped to handle both.

However, know that no person is immune to the erosive ebb tides of temptation, fatigue and fear. We're all vulnerable.

And as Bobby Dylan sang, in need of guidance and strength upon which to anchor our decisions and true our course:

"Don't let me drift too far. Keep me where you are, where I will always be renewed."

Five decades ago, roasting under gown-and-cap in the Ohio sun, my goal was survival. On that day, "long-range" was about ninety minutes. The five decades ahead never crossed my mind.

And now, suddenly, it seems they've become my last fifty years. A half-century "blur"—posing familiar questions: "How did so much time pass so quickly? Where did the years go? Was it all it should have been?"

So expect the same: that you'll burn through your next fifty years, likely at an accelerating pace; and, that it'll happen fast.

So seize each moment. Commit to doing the right thing. Persevere. And always give back more than you get.

And waste no time hugging tree trunks. Like good fruit, the best version of you will always grow at the end of the bough. Out past the familiar, easy and comfortable.

To become all you can be, you must crawl far out on the limb, to a place Mark Knopfler calls "...at the edge of the night, still a light that gleams, beyond your wildest dreams."

I'll close by wishing you calm seas, a following wind, and a noble run—years lived fully...

And upon completion, a grateful world weeping its loss...

Even as you rejoice, the time you were granted.

Liquid Tarmac
I Was Sure I Could Do It!

As you've discovered, *BULLSEYE!* delivers multiple important lessons for life and business. Plus, at its core, it's always a book about "belief."

For if that man in 1972, didn't believe he could hit the bullseye, because he was blind, this book and one of the most popular and impactful stories I tell, wouldn't exist.

And now, when I speak to a group, to reinforce the importance and significance of belief, I tell an additional story. While I keep searching for a better story about "belief" since 2009, I can't find one. So I'll continue to stick with and tell this one.

* * * * *

January 15, 2009, New York City was chilly. That morning, a light one-inch snowfall. High temperature, 22 degrees.

3:26 P.M. Wheels up. US Airways flight 1549 had just taken off from New York's LaGuardia airport. Headed for Charlotte, North Carolina. It was under the leadership of Captain Chesley "Sully" Sullenberger III, who brought into play that afternoon decades of experience as a veteran commercial aviator, Air Force fighter pilot, and glider pilot.

3:28 P.M. A harrowing Canadian geese bird strike hits flight 1549's windscreen and two engines. Sully sees the damage. Feels the vibrations. Smells the destruction. Both engines disabled. All thrust lost—at low speed, low altitude. And over a densely populated city.

Sully quickly determined a return to LaGuardia was problematic and likely, catastrophic. So he glances to the right and considers landing at New Jersey's Teterboro Airport. He realizes that won't work either.

So he now banks left, and stares at New York's Hudson River. And decides to turn the Hudson, into a liquid tarmac. (It became his bullseye.)

While it's true that tough times call for tough people, those who are tough, are among the best prepared, best trained and best believers. (For if you don't believe, nobody else will.)

Sully decides and informs air traffic control, "We're going in the Hudson." (A decision made two-and-a-half minutes into the flight and one minute after the bird strike.)

He then informs his crew and passengers in a cabin announcement, "Brace for impact." The flight attendants immediately, repeatedly and in unison, encourage passengers to, "Heads down. Stay down. Heads down. Stay down."

3:31 P.M. Thanks to Sully's amazing, dramatic and stunningly spectacular performance, he successfully ditched, or "landed," flight 1549 in New York's Hudson River. A landing he described as "A gentle glide."

Have you heard the cockpit recordings? Remarkable. His voice, calm. Controlled. Decisive.

Did he know the risks? The potential for failure? Of course. Was he thinking about them? Apparently not!

When Sully was asked by CBS television-news journalist Katie Couric, "If he was afraid of not making it..." he answered, "I was sure I could do it."

Because he knew he could do it, plus, had the teamwork of first officer co-pilot Jeff Skiles and flight attendants Donna Dent, Doreen Welsh and Sheila Dail, 155 lives were saved. On the plane! (150 passengers and 5 crew members.) Imagine the number of lives potentially saved in Manhattan office and residential buildings or on-the-ground.

To Sully the Hudson was *THE* viable choice. The alternative with the greatest likelihood for success. It was no longer a river. It became a liquid tarmac. An aquatic landing strip.

Sully also told Couric, "His entire life was preparation for that moment."

And here's what he had to prepare for...

Sully stressed when the airplane touched the water the nose had to be slightly up, the wings exactly level, the descent rate acceptable, with a flying speed just above minimum flying speed and not below it.

BULLSEYE!

And they *all* had to be done at the same time.

Yet, once again, Sully *knew* he could do it.

With what's before you...

Personally or professionally...

Can you do it?

I know, you know...

That *you* too...

Can do it!

About the Author

HELPING OTHERS WIN BIG! Those who want to win BIG in today's competitive marketplace call Jeff Blackman. He's a speaker, author, success coach, broadcast personality, and lawyer. He heads Blackman & Associates—a results-producing business-growth firm in the Chicagoland area.

Jeff's clients call him a "business-growth specialist." His customized *Referrals: Your Road to Results* learning system helped one financial services client generate $230 million directly from referrals in only 23 months!

DELIVERS RESULTS! Since 1985, Jeff has shared his positive and profit-producing messages with numerous Fortune 500 companies, closely-held businesses, entrepreneurial-driven organizations and association audiences throughout the world.

Whether Jeff works with you once, or once-a-month in an on-going learning-system, he helps you outdistance your competition and reach new levels of unprecedented success. His high-energy and high-content messages have immediate take-home value.

HALL OF FAMER, AWARD WINNER, HONORS. On August 4, 2008, in New York City, Jeff was inducted into the National Speakers

Association's *Speaker Hall of Fame*. He was awarded the *CPAE: Council of Peers Award for Excellence* designation. To date, only 264 professional or celebrity speakers have been selected and honored worldwide, including; Ronald Reagan, Colin Powell, Zig Ziglar, and Norman Vincent Peale.

Jeff is also one of approximately thirteen percent of professional speakers to receive the CSP or *Certified Speaking Professional* designation from NSA. And in June, 2008, Vistage, the world's leading CEO organization, named Jeff *Fast Track Speaker of the Year*, based upon the quality and impact of his content and delivery. Jeff also graduated with honors from both the University of Illinois and the Illinois Institute of Technology Chicago Kent College of Law.

BESTSELLING AUTHOR. Jeff's bestselling books include: *Opportunity \$elling®*, *RESULT\$*, *Carpe A.M. • Carpe P.M. – Seize Your Destiny™*, *Peak Your Profits,* (an Amazon bestseller)—which was also published in China, Malaysia and Singapore, and selected by Fast Track as one of "the best business books on tape" and, *Stop Whining! Start Selling!*, which achieved "Bestseller" status at Amazon within one month of its release.

As an audio-author, Jeff's results-strategies were featured on Nightingale-Conant's *Sound Selling*. POPP Publishing released/distributes Jeff's audio business-growth system: *Opportunity \$elling®* - Six Profit-Producing Steps to Multiply Your Earnings and the *RESULT\$* CD. Jeff has also written and hosts two video learning-systems published by JWA Video; *Profitable Customer Service* and *How to Set and Really Achieve Your Goals*.

BROADCASTER. As a radio and TV talk-show host, some of Jeff's guests have been: Oprah Winfrey, Jerry Seinfeld, Albert Brooks, Penn Jillette, astronaut Jim Lovell and Olympic gold medalist Bruce Jenner.

HAPPY HUSBAND. DEVOTED FATHER. NEW GRANDFATHER. NUTTY FAN. Jeff is a happy husband, devoted father, ecstatic new grandfather, veteran softball player, avid biker, and a loyal or nutty Chicago Cubs fan. He and his family are also crazy Chicago Blackhawks, Bears and Bulls fans. (They also love the Cubs, yet over the years, (aside from 2016), have spent lots of time consoling Jeff!) On Sunday nights, the Blackmans can often be spotted together at a local hip, happenin' or dive restaurant eating, talking, and laughing!

Blackman & Associates, LLC
2105 Dauntless Drive • Glenview, IL 60026
Phone: 847.998.0688 • Fax: 847.998.0675
jeff@jeffblackman.com • www.jeffblackman.com

Visit Jeff's website and subscribe to his FREE e-letter, *The Results Report*. Plus connect with Jeff on LinkedIn and Facebook and follow him on Twitter: @BlackmanResults

If you'd like to see Jeff *tell* the bullseye story, please go to ResultsTV and his Vintage Video Vault at https://www.jeffblackman.com then click on *Staying on Target*

What do YOU think?
Your opinion matters!
A polite request.

Valued reader,

Yea! Way to go! You finished! I'm proud of you.

Hope you enjoyed and had as much fun reading *Bullseye!* as I had writing it. May it continue to be a source of inspiration, results and growth—in your personal and professional lives.

Am always here for you. So our relationship should continue to grow. Meaning, if I can be of help to you in any way, please look at me as your "go-to-guy." You're welcome to shoot me an email at jeff@ jeffblackman.com or buzz me at: 847.998.0688.

Also, since your opinion is important and really matters, I could sure use your help. It would mean a lot to me, and future readers, if you could please take just a few minutes and write a quick review of *Bullseye!* on Amazon. What did you especially like? How did it help or inspire you? What actions did you take or results are you already achieving?

Your honest input and experience will help others attain new levels of success. Thanks a lot! Really appreciate it.

May you continue to hit your bullseye—at home and at work!

Keynotes, Coaching, Workshops and Learning-Systems by Jeff Blackman

DRIVE GROWTH AND RESULTS. Jeff:

- Ignites and inspires you to attain new levels of success.
- Helps you outdistance your competition.
- Enhances your performance, productivity and profitability.
- Accelerates your growth.
- Dramatically increases your results.

Unique, creative, honest, hard-hitting, and humorous, Jeff's customized high-content, results-oriented, and profit-producing messages in sales, marketing, negotiations, customer service, leadership and change have immediate application. If you hire speakers or influence the selection of speakers at your company or professional association, please contact Jeff to learn more about how he can help you, your team, or members hit your bullseyes and peak your profits!

What do clients value most about Jeff? His:

- Energy and quick connection with an audience.
- Quality content and real-world solutions.
- Warm, friendly, and impactful style.
- Commitment to customization and exhaustive research.
- Focus on quantifiable, measurable results and outcomes.
- Powerful, profit-producing messages.

- Sense of humor and spontaneity.
- Positive, fun, and meaningful audience interaction.
- Dedication to long-term success with ongoing reinforcement.

Plus, he's fun and easy to work with!

To maximize your results, please contact:
Sheryl Kantor • Director of Marketing
Blackman & Associates, LLC
sheryl@jeffblackman.com • 847.998.0688
www.jeffblackman.com

Also by Jeff Blackman

Peak Your Profits!® book

Stop Whining! Start Selling! book

RESULT$ book plus audio

Carpe A.M. • *Carpe P.M. / Seize Your Destiny*™ book

Opportunity $elling® / *Your Path to Profit*® book

Opportunity $elling® audio business-growth system

Profitable Customer Service video

How to Set and Really Achieve Your Goals video

Opportunity $elling® *Style Analysis* assessments
Management Style Analysis assessments
Customer Service Style Analysis assessments

A-to-Z, Be the Best You Can Be! inspirational tools

Please see www.jeffblackman.com and click on:
"Business-Growth Tools"

SPECIAL BULLSEYE BONUS

Would you like to receive a PDF with some
bonus *Bullseye Breakthroughs & Boosters*?
For free? Of course you would!

Simply send an email to: sheryl@jeffblackman.com
with the subject heading: Bullseye B&B

Acknowledgments

To my family, I love each of you—more than you'll ever know.

Am grateful to the many clients, radio and TV talk-show guests, friends, family, teachers and influencers—who have enabled me to succeed, personally and professionally.

Thanks to the man who gave me the opportunity to witness his bullseye achievement. Although I'll never know you or your name, you've had a profound impact on my life. And you're the inspiration for one of my most popular signature stories and this book.

My pals and lifelong friends at the National Speakers Association—for giving me an incredibly smart international network of friends and advisors.

The Chicago Cubs—who always hold my heart in their hands—and still try to convince me, the next championship drought—won't be another 108 years!

Here's to...

Your next bullseye...

As you hit your targets,
at home and at work!

Manufactured by Amazon.ca
Acheson, AB

12852576R00070